T0387627

WHO'S HOO? OWLS!

Barn Owls

by Elizabeth Neuenfeldt

BELLWETHER MEDIA • MINNEAPOLIS, MN

Blastoff! Readers are carefully developed by literacy experts to build reading stamina and move students toward fluency by combining standards-based content with developmentally appropriate text.

 **Level 1** provides the most support through repetition of high-frequency words, light text, predictable sentence patterns, and strong visual support.

 **Level 2** offers early readers a bit more challenge through varied sentences, increased text load, and text-supportive special features.

 **Level 3** advances early-fluent readers toward fluency through increased text load, less reliance on photos, advancing concepts, longer sentences, and more complex special features.

★ **Blastoff! Universe**

Reading Level

Blastoff! Beginners — Grade K

Blastoff! Readers — Grades 1–3

Blastoff! Discovery — Grade 4

This edition first published in 2024 by Bellwether Media, Inc.

No part of this publication may be reproduced in whole or in part without written permission of the publisher. For information regarding permission, write to Bellwether Media, Inc., Attention: Permissions Department, 6012 Blue Circle Drive, Minnetonka, MN 55343.

Library of Congress Cataloging-in-Publication Data

Names: Neuenfeldt, Elizabeth, author.
Title: Barn owls / by Elizabeth Neuenfeldt.
Description: Minneapolis, MN : Bellwether Media, Inc., 2024. | Series: Blastoff! Readers. Who's hoo? Owls! | Includes bibliographical references and index. | Audience: Ages 5-8 | Audience: Grades 2-3 | Summary: "Relevant images match informative text in this introduction to barn owls. Intended for students in kindergarten through third grade"-- Provided by publisher.
Identifiers: LCCN 2023008920 (print) | LCCN 2023008921 (ebook) | ISBN 9798886874129 (library binding) | ISBN 9798886876000 (ebook)
Subjects: LCSH: Barn owl--Juvenile literature.
Classification: LCC QL696.S85 N48 2024 (print) | LCC QL696.S85 (ebook) | DDC 598.9/7--dc23/eng/20230309
LC record available at https://lccn.loc.gov/2023008920
LC ebook record available at https://lccn.loc.gov/2023008921

Editor: Rebecca Sabelko   Designer: Brittany McIntosh

Printed in the United States of America, North Mankato, MN.

Table of **Contents**

Owls in Barns

Barn owls are found all around the world!

They are known for resting in barns during the day.

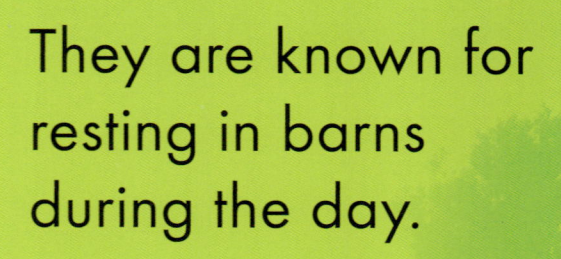

Barn Owl Range

N
W E
S

range = ☐

Barn owls have white, heart-shaped faces.

6

short, sharp beak

Their eyes are big and dark.
Their beaks are short and sharp.

Barn owls have gray and brownish-yellow wings.

The feathers on their chests are light. Females also have dark brown spots.

Spot a Barn Owl!

heart-shaped face

big, dark eyes

dark brown spots (females)

Barn owls are medium-sized. Some grow almost 16 inches (41 centimeters) tall.

Their **wingspan** can stretch up to 4 feet (1.2 meters) wide!

Barn Owl Wingspan

0 1 foot 2 feet 3 feet 4 feet

up to 4 feet (1.2 meters) wide

Silent Hunters

Barn owls hunt at night.
They fly low over open areas
to find food.

Their soft, light feathers help them fly silently.

13

Barn owls have excellent hearing and eyesight. They can easily find **prey**.

They catch small **mammals** with their sharp **talons**. They eat some food whole!

rodent

Barn Owl Food

rabbits

voles

talons

15

Sometimes other large **raptors** attack barn owls.

predator

Barn owls try to scare **predators** to stay safe. They hiss and flap their wings.

17

Life of a Barn Owl

tree cavity

Barn owls **roost** during the day. They rest in **cavities** inside barns, caves, and trees.

18

They live alone or in pairs.

roosting in a barn

19

Female barn owls lay up to 18 eggs! **Owlets** break out of eggs after one month.

Owlets become **fledglings** in about two months. They are ready to fly!

owlet

Growing Up

1 egg
about 1 month

2 owlet
about 2 months

3 fledgling
10 months

life span: 2 to 4 years

Glossary

cavities—holes or spaces inside of things

fledglings—young owls that have feathers for flight

mammals—warm-blooded animals that have backbones and feed their young milk

owlets—baby owls

predators—animals that hunt other animals for food

prey—animals that are hunted by other animals for food

raptors—birds that hunt other animals; raptors have excellent eyesight and powerful talons.

roost—to rest or sleep

talons—the strong, sharp claws of owls and other raptors

wingspan—the distance from the tip of one wing to the tip of the other wing

To Learn More

AT THE LIBRARY

Andrews, Elizabeth. *Barn Owls*. Minneapolis, Minn.: Pop!, 2023.

Barnes, Rachael. *Great Horned Owls*. Minneapolis, Minn.: Bellwether Media, 2024.

Clausen-Grace, Nicki. *Owls*. Mankato, Minn.: Black Rabbit Books, 2019.

ON THE WEB

FACTSURFER.com gives you a safe, fun way to find more information.

1. Go to www.factsurfer.com.

2. Enter "barn owls" into the search box and click 🔍.

3. Select your book cover to see a list of related content.

Index

The images in this book are reproduced through the courtesy of: Eric Isselee, front cover, pp. 9 (main, inset), 11, 22; Michael Shake, p. 3; Vlada Cech, p. 4; Rachel Swallow, p. 6; Susan E. Degginger/ Alamy, p. 7 (top); Abeselom Zerit, p. 7 (bottom); Monika Surzin, p. 8; Dagmara Ksandrova, p. 10; Steven Ward, p. 12; Suzanne Renfrow, p. 13; Albert Beukhof, pp. 14, 20; MZPHOTO.CZ, pp. 14-15; Tom Reichner, p. 15 (top left); Agnieszka Bacal, p. 15 (top right); Carol Gray, p. 16; Stanislav Judas, p. 17; Alan Walker/ Getty Images, p. 18; Dennis Astroth, p. 19; BBA Photography, pp. 20-21; David Hosking/ Alamy, p. 21 (top left); reathe163, p. 21 (top middle); Christopher Chambers, p. 21 (top right).

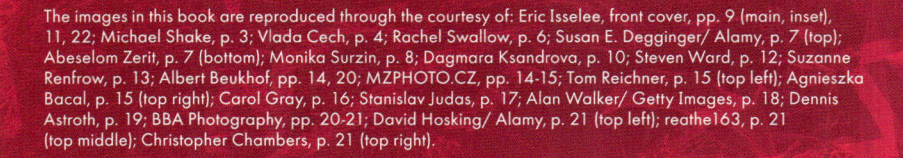